D0653837

CHARLES DARWIN

Sarah Ridley

W

FRANKLIN WATTS

LONDON • SYDNEY

First published in 2014 by Franklin Watts

Copyright © Franklin Watts 2014

Franklin Watts
338 Euston Road
London NW1 3BH

Franklin Watts Australia
Level 17/207 Kent Street
Sydney, NSW 2000

Editor in chief: John C. Miles
Design: Jonathan Hair and Matt Lilly
Art director: Peter Scoulding
Picture research: Diana Morris
Original design concept: Sophie Williams

Picture credits: Antiquarian Images/MEPL: 9. Colin Boycott/
Dreamstime: 17cr. Cambridge University Library: 15. Richard
Carter/Flickr. CC. Some rights reserved: 6. HMS Beagle in the
Galapagos, by John Chancellor (1925-1984), courtesy of Gordon
Chancellor: 8. Christ's College Cambridge: 4. English Heritage/HIP/
Getty Images: 21. The Granger Collection/Topfoto: 18. MEPL: 10.
NHMPL: 11, 13, 14, 16, 23. Oxford Science Archive/HIP/Topfoto:
22. Photoresearchers/MEPL: 5. powerofforever/istockphotos: 12.
University of Cambridge Zoology Museum: 7. CC.
Wikimedia Commons: front cover, 19, 20.
*Every attempt has been made to clear copyright. Should there be any
inadvertent omission please apply to the publisher for rectification.*

Dewey number: 576.8'2'092
HB ISBN 978 1 4451 3055 2
Library ebook ISBN 978 1 4451 3063 7

Printed in China

Franklin Watts is a division of Hachette Children's Books,
an Hachette UK company.

www.hachette.co.uk

Contents

A country childhood

Charles Darwin was born over two hundred years ago in Shropshire, England. His father was a successful doctor and the family were wealthy. Charles lived with his family and often visited his cousins nearby.

Charles grew up in The Mount, Shrewsbury in Shropshire.

1809-1825

A portrait of Charles, aged six, with his sister Catherine.

1796

Robert Darwin marries Susannah Wedgwood, daughter of the potter, Josiah Wedgwood.

12 February 1809

Charles Darwin is born, the fifth of six children.

1817

His mother dies when he is eight.

1818–25

He attends boarding school in Shrewsbury.

At school, Charles found studying Latin and Greek rather boring. Back at home, he was at his happiest wandering around the garden or walking in the countryside. He collected rocks, shells and insects and also enjoyed hunting animals and shooting birds.

To university

Charles went to Edinburgh University to study medicine but he hated it. After two years, his father decided that Charles might do better as a vicar and sent him to study theology at Cambridge University instead.

Charles' room at Christ's College, Cambridge.

1825–27

Charles studies medicine at Edinburgh University.

1827–31

He studies theology (religious beliefs) at Cambridge University.

1830

Charles Lyell's book *The Principles of Geology* is published.

1825-1831

Charles collected beetles and displayed them in special boxes and drawers.

Charles actually spent his time studying insects and rocks instead. He went on trips into the countryside with his friends, collecting beetles. He learnt how to study in a scientific way from professors who were experts in rocks and plants.

EXPERIMENT

Make your own natural history collection. Use a camera to take photos of wild flowers. Record where you found them and use a field guide to identify them. Or make a collection of leaves or shells and use a field guide to help you label them correctly.

1831

Charles Darwin finishes his degree in theology.

1831

On a trip to Wales, he studies rocks with Professor Sedgwick.

1831

He is offered the chance to go on a voyage.

All aboard HMS *Beagle*

27 December 1831

The voyage of HMS *Beagle* begins.

January 1832

Darwin lands on the Cape Verde Islands in the Atlantic Ocean and notices a layer of shells high up a cliff.

HMS Beagle *set out with a crew of 73.*

February 1832

The ship reaches the coast of South America.

When Charles Darwin was invited to join a voyage on board HMS *Beagle*, he leapt at the chance. His job was to study plants and animals, and to keep the captain company. The main reason for the voyage was to map the coastline of South America.

Over the next five years, the ship sailed across the Atlantic Ocean to South America, and then on to the Galapagos Islands, New Zealand, Australia and South Africa. Out at sea, Darwin felt seasick. He spent his time reading, including a book about rocks by Charles Lyell, which had a great influence on him.

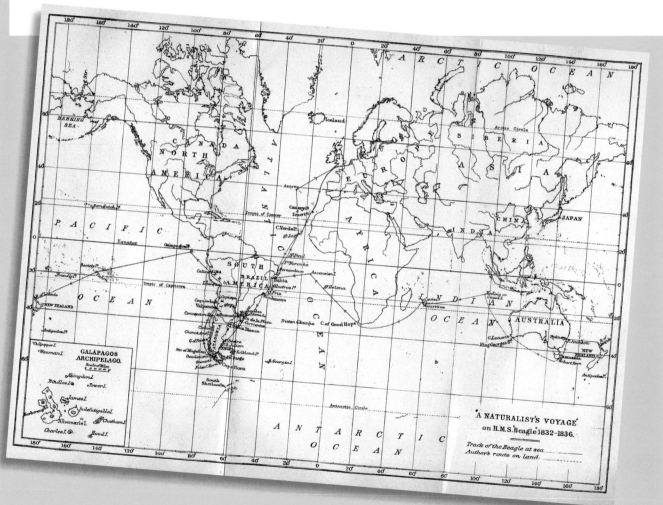

HMS Beagle's voyage was supposed to take two years, but actually lasted almost five.

1832–35

HMS *Beagle* travels up and down the coast of South America.

1832

In South America Darwin finds fossils of a huge armadillo-like creature and eats a much smaller, modern-day armadillo for dinner.

1835

In Chile he sees a volcano erupt and experiences an earthquake.

At this time, many people believed that God created the world in six days, about six thousand years earlier. Some scientists, including Charles Lyell, thought this couldn't be so because of the evidence contained in ancient fossils and rocks.

Charles Lyell believed that the Earth was millions of years old.

Some of the shells that Darwin collected and identified on his trip.

On the voyage, Darwin was free to explore when the *Beagle* dropped anchor. He collected rocks, shells and fossils and recorded where he found them in his notebooks. Everything he saw pointed towards Lyell being right – the Earth really is millions of years old.

BREAKTHROUGH

Darwin used scientific skills to carefully record and identify the rock samples he collected. He also used a microscope and other tools, so that he could look at their structure. His skill as a geologist helped improve his career as a scientist when he returned to England.

Darwin the collector

During the voyage, Darwin was amazed by the variety of animals and plants he saw in South America and the Galapagos Islands. His job was to describe them and collect specimens to send back to England. This he did, collecting over 5,000 specimens, all carefully labelled and described in notebooks.

Darwin saw iguanas, like these ones that are basking on the rocks of the Galapagos Islands.

1832–36

Back in Cambridge, Professor Henslow unpacks Darwin's specimens and publishes some of his letters.

1835

Darwin investigates coral reefs.

September/October 1835

On the Galapagos Islands, he sees a huge variety of animals and plants, including iguanas and giant tortoises.

1831–1836

To keep in touch with family and friends, Darwin wrote hundreds of letters. He also wrote to experts, asking for advice on how to preserve his specimens. He dried some, pressed others, put them in jars of wine, stuffed them and packed them in boxes to send back to England.

One of the beetles Darwin collected and labelled during the voyage.

BREAKTHROUGH

Darwin saw types (species) of animals and plants that were closely related to each other and yet were different. He wondered whether a species always stays the same, or whether it might actually change over a long period of time.

November 1835

In Tahiti, he notices the beauty of the island but he also feels homesick.

late 1835–early 1836

He visits New Zealand and Australia.

October 1836

HMS *Beagle* sails back to England.

After almost five years, HMS *Beagle* finally arrived back in England. Darwin set to work sorting out his notes and his specimens. Experts helped him and took a great interest in what he had found. At this time, Darwin began to suffer pain and sickness that no doctor knew how to cure. Despite this, he carried on working.

In different parts of Patagonia, Darwin saw small and big rheas, huge birds similar to ostriches.

In 1837 he sketched the outline of a big new idea. He thought that maybe plants and animals did not stay the same but evolved, or changed, over time. This might explain how an armadillo could be related to its giant fossil ancestor.

1836–82

Darwin is ill, on and off, for the rest of his life.

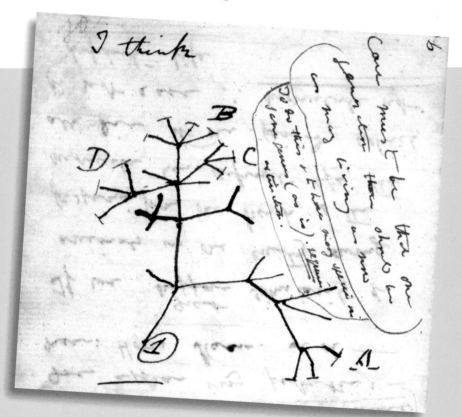

1836–43

He works with others to publish *The Zoology of the Voyage of the Beagle*.

BREAKTHROUGH

Drawn in 1837, Darwin's Tree of Life sketch shows a branching tree, linking living animals and plants with a shared ancestor, as well as species that have died out. How could this be? Gradually Darwin worked out the answer – his theory of evolution by natural selection.

1837

He sketches the Tree of Life. He only talks to his two closest friends, Charles Lyell and Joseph Hooker, about the idea.

Proving the idea

In secret, Darwin kept developing his ideas. He saw that tiny differences (variations) between, for instance, baby rabbits, could give them a better chance of surviving by passing on this advantage to their young. Over many generations, these tiny variations can become more obvious, and could result in a new species. He called this idea "evolution by natural selection".

BREAKTHROUGH

A bird expert noticed that Darwin had labelled small birds from the Galapagos Islands as different species when they were in fact all finches. Darwin gradually realised that each type of finch came from a different island and that their beak had evolved to feed on food available there – insects, berries or seeds.

Darwin's finches from the Galapagos Islands.

1837

Queen Victoria becomes queen.

1839

Darwin marries Emma Wedgwood. They have ten children together. He publishes his diary of the voyage.

1842

He publishes a book about coral reefs. The Darwin family moves to Down House, Kent.

At the same time, he got on with the rest of his life. In 1839 he married his cousin, Emma Wedgwood. The Darwins moved to Down House, the perfect place for them to bring up a large family and for Charles to think and write in peace.

Darwin lived at Down House for over forty years.

1842–44

He writes down his ideas on evolution by natural selection.

1846–54

He becomes an expert on barnacles and publishes a book about them.

1855–58

He breeds pigeons as part of his research on evolution.

On the Origin of Species

June 1858

Darwin receives Wallace's letter. It is a difficult time for Darwin as his youngest son is ill and then dies.

July 1858

Wallace and Darwin's ideas about evolution are presented to the Linnean Society in London.

November 1859

On the Origin of Species is published and sells out on the first day.

Darwin continued with his secret studies but spent most of his time writing other books. This was all to change when he received a letter from Alfred Russel Wallace in 1858, describing his ideas about evolution by natural selection – and they matched Darwin's. Darwin was stunned.

Alfred Russel Wallace collected thousands of insects during long trips abroad.

ON

THE ORIGIN OF SPECIES

BY MEANS OF NATURAL SELECTION,

OR THE

PRESERVATION OF FAVOURED RACES IN THE STRUGGLE
FOR LIFE.

By CHARLES DARWIN, M.A.,

FELLOW OF THE ROYAL, GEOLOGICAL, LINNÆAN, ETC., SOCIETIES;
AUTHOR OF 'JOURNAL OF RESEARCHES DURING H. M. S. BEAGLE'S VOYAGE
ROUND THE WORLD.'

LONDON:
JOHN MURRAY, ALBEMARLE STREET.
1859.

The right of Translation is reserved.

Darwin decided that the fair thing to do was to make an announcement presenting both their ideas. He also realised that he must publish his own work on evolution – and quickly. He set about writing a short book and published it with the title *On the Origin of Species.*

The title page for On The Origin of Species *by Charles Darwin.*

Darwin's book created a storm. It upset many religious people who believed that God had created all animals and plants as we see them today. Newspapers published stories for and against his ideas. Despite this, it sold thousands of copies and made Darwin famous.

After the publication of The Descent of Man *in 1871, in which Darwin wrote that apes and human beings shared ancestors, this cartoon was published showing an orangutan with Darwin's head.*

1859–60

People debate the ideas in Darwin's book in newspapers and at meetings.

1861–62

Darwin grows orchids and writes about them.

1865

He publishes a book about plants.

Darwin spent most of his later life at Down House, enjoying family life and the peace of his garden and surrounding area. He took regular walks along a sandy path, which he named 'my thinking path'.

This photo of Darwin was taken outside his home, a year before his death.

1871	**1872**	**1875–80**	**1876**
His book, *The Descent of Man*, upsets even more people.	He publishes a book about human and animal emotions.	He is researching and writing about plants.	He writes a memoir for his children.

A great scientist

Darwin's interest in the natural world continued up to his death. At the end of his life he was fascinated by worms and the way they recycle dead plant material into the soil. At the age of 73 he died at home, surrounded by his family.

Darwin's family were persuaded to hold Darwin's funeral in Westminster Abbey.

1881	**19 April 1882**	**1885**
Darwin publishes his book about worms.	Charles Darwin dies, aged 73. His funeral is held in Westminster Abbey, attended by important people.	A statue of Charles Darwin is unveiled at the Natural History Museum in London.

1881 to now

Darwin was a brilliant scientist whose big idea, evolution by natural selection, changed the way people think about life on Earth. Evolution is taught in schools and universities worldwide. Now most people accept that all life is related to the most ancient early forms of life. The study of DNA has proved this to be true.

A statue of Charles Darwin looks down on all who enter the Natural History Museum in London.

1909

Scientists gather in Cambridge to celebrate the 100th anniversary of his birth.

2009

All around the world, people celebrate the 200th anniversary of his birth.

Glossary

ancestor An individual living thing that lived in the past, and from whom other individuals are descended.

barnacle A tiny animal that lives in the sea and has a shell.

coral reef A solid underwater structure made up of the skeletons of tiny animals.

DNA Deoxyribonucleic acid. This material carries all the information about how a living thing will look and function.

evolution The process of change over time.

fossil The trace of an animal or plant, preserved in rock.

Galapagos Islands Ten main islands and several smaller ones in the Pacific Ocean.

geologist Someone who studies rocks and the structure of the Earth.

HMS His/Her Majesty's Service.

natural history Animals and plants, and the study of them.

natural selection How individual living things that are best suited to where they live will be more likely to survive and pass on any natural advantage to their offspring.

naturalist Someone who studies plants and animals.

professor A high ranking teacher at a university.

species A group of living things that are very similar and are able to breed. (There are 5,416 species of mammal. Of these, two are species of elephant.)

theology The study of God and religious beliefs.

voyage A long sea or space journey.

Index